SENEGAL 2016 HUMAN RIGHTS REPORT

EXECUTIVE SUMMARY

Senegal is a republic dominated by a strong executive branch. In 2012 voters elected Macky Sall to succeed Abdoulaye Wade as president for a seven-year term. In 2012 Sall's coalition won a majority of seats in the National Assembly. Local and international observers viewed the elections as largely free and fair.

Civilian authorities generally maintained effective control over the security forces.

The most significant human rights problems included harsh prison conditions, lengthy pretrial detention, and discrimination and violence against women, including rape and female genital mutilation/cutting (FGM/C).

Other major human rights problems included security force abuse, including torture, arbitrary arrest, questionable investigative detention, and lack of judicial independence. Corruption--particularly in the judiciary, police, and executive branch--was a problem. Child abuse, early and forced marriage, infanticide, and trafficking in persons occurred. Violence and discrimination against lesbian, gay, bisexual, transgender, and intersex (LGBTI) persons continued, as did discrimination against persons with HIV/AIDS. Forced labor, including by children, was a problem.

The government took steps to investigate, prosecute, and punish officials who committed abuses, whether in the security forces or elsewhere in the government, but impunity existed.

In the southern Casamance region, situated between The Gambia and Guinea-Bissau, a de facto ceasefire between security forces and armed separatists continued for a fourth year. Gunmen associated with various factions of the separatist Movement of Democratic Forces of the Casamance (MFDC), however, continued to rob and harass local populations. While there were occasional unplanned skirmishes between security forces and MFDC units, neither side conducted offensive operations. Mediation efforts continued in search of a negotiated resolution of the conflict, which began in 1982.

Section 1. Respect for the Integrity of the Person, Including Freedom from:

a. Arbitrary Deprivation of Life and other Unlawful or Politically Motivated

Killings

There was at least one report the government or its agents committed arbitrary or unlawful killings.

On March 17, Paul Prince Johnson, a foreign detainee, died in prison in the city of Diourbel. Amnesty International, the Senegalese Human Rights League, and the International Society for Human Rights reported allegations that Johnson died from inhuman and cruel treatment by prison guards. Despite their calls for an independent investigation, none had been conducted by year's end, and the government's post-mortem examination attributed Johnson's death to natural causes.

On June 24, a court in Dakar sentenced police officer Mouhamed Boughaleb to 20 years of hard labor for the 2014 shooting death of student demonstrator Bassirou Faye.

In July a criminal court in the city of Mbacke convicted four police officers-- Thiendella Ndiaye, Waly Almamy Toure, Mame Kor Ngong, and Ousmane Ndao-- of violence and assault following the 2013 death of Ibrahama Samb, a bus conductor who died in police custody while being transported to a police station in the locked trunk of a car. The court also ordered the government to pay compensation up to 20 million CFA francs ($34,000) to Samb's family. There was no indication the government had paid the compensation by year's end.

b. Disappearance

There were no reports of politically motivated disappearances.

c. Torture and Other Cruel, Inhuman, or Degrading Treatment or Punishment

The constitution and law prohibit such practices, but there were occasional reports government officials employed them.

Human rights organizations noted examples of physical abuse committed by law enforcement, including cruel and degrading treatment in prisons and detention facilities. In particular, they criticized strip search and interrogation methods. Police reportedly forced detainees to sleep on bare floors, directed bright lights at them, beat them with batons, and kept them in cells with minimal access to fresh air. The government claimed these practices were not widespread and that it usually conducted formal investigations into allegations of abuse. Investigations, however, often were unduly prolonged and rarely resulted in charges or indictments.

On July 29, the Appellate Chamber of the Criminal Court of Dakar acquitted Cheikh Diop and Cheikh Sidaty Mane, who were sentenced in 2015 to 20 years' imprisonment in connection with the 2012 lynching of Fode Ndiaye, a police officer. Ndiaye was killed in clashes between police and opposition supporters holding a peaceful rally to protest former president Wade's attempt to stand for a third term. According to Amnesty International, Diop and Sidaty were convicted despite their statements police had tortured them into confessing. In a statement to the press after their release, the two men reiterated their allegations of torture. Amnesty called on authorities to investigate, but no investigation had been initiated by year's end.

Prison and Detention Center Conditions

Prison and detention center conditions were harsh and potentially life threatening due to food shortages, overcrowding, poor sanitation, and inadequate medical care.

Physical Conditions: Overcrowding was endemic. For example, Dakar's main prison facility, Rebeuss, held more than twice the number of inmates for which it was designed. Female detainees generally had better conditions than did men. Pretrial detainees were not always separated from convicted prisoners. Juvenile boys were often housed with men or permitted to roam freely with men during the day. Girls were held together with women. Infants and newborns were often kept in prison with their mothers until age one, with no special cells, additional medical provisions, or extra food rations.

In addition to overcrowding, the National Organization for Human Rights, a nongovernmental organization (NGO), identified lack of adequate sanitation as a major problem. Poor and insufficient food, limited access to medical care, stifling heat, poor drainage, and insect infestations also were problems throughout the prison system.

On March 28, four juvenile detainees at Rebeuss Prison went on a hunger strike to protest lengthy pretrial detention and poor prison conditions. The government subsequently increased the daily allotment for prisoner food and care to 680 CFA francs ($1.15) in all prisons. Despite the increase, prison conditions remained unsatisfactory. In late August several prisoners in Kaolack engaged in a hunger strike to protest conditions. In September hundreds of prisoners in Rebeuss engaged in a two-week hunger strike to protest lengthy pretrial detention and poor prison conditions. This hunger strike culminated in a September 20 prison riot, during which at least one prisoner died. On September 21, in solidarity with their fellow inmates in Rebeuss, prisoners in Thies engaged in a one-day hunger strike. Following these incidents, authorities announced they would construct additional prison facilities and hire additional prison staff.

According to 2014 government statistics, the most recent available, 50 inmates died in prisons and detention centers in 2014.

Administration: Authorities did not always conduct credible investigations into allegations of mistreatment. In 2014, however, prisoner complaints of harsh treatment prompted at least two inspections by the National Prevention Mechanism, which subsequently criticized living conditions and lengthy pretrial detention. The inspection resulted in the filing of criminal charges against two prison officials, and the case continued at year's end.

Prison officials kept some records on prisoners and detainees, but computerized records were inaccurate due to inadequate staff training and power shortages at many government facilities. Authorities did not use alternatives for sentencing nonviolent offenders. Ombudsmen were available to respond to complaints, but prisoners did not know how to access them or file reports. Prisoners generally had reasonable access to visitors and some access to lawyers, and they could observe religious practices. Unlike in previous years, authorities permitted prisoners and detainees to submit complaints to judicial authorities without censorship and to request investigation of credible allegations of inhuman conditions, but there was no evidence that officials conducted any follow-up investigations.

Independent Monitoring: The government permitted prison visits by local human rights groups, all of which operated independently, and international observers. The National Observer of Detention Facilities had full and unfettered access to all civilian prison and detention facilities, but not to military and intelligence facilities. The observer published an annual report, although the 2015 report had not been published by year's end.

Members of the International Committee of the Red Cross visited prisons in Dakar and the Casamance.

d. Arbitrary Arrest or Detention

The constitution and law prohibit arbitrary arrest and detention; however, the government did not always observe these prohibitions.

Role of the Police and Security Apparatus

Police and gendarmes are responsible for maintaining law and order. The army shares that responsibility in exceptional cases, such as during a state of emergency. The National Police are part of the Interior Ministry and operate in major cities. The Gendarmerie is part of the Ministry of Defense and primarily operates outside of major cities.

Civilian authorities generally maintained effective control over police, gendarmes, and the army, but the government did not have effective mechanisms to punish abuse and corruption. The Criminal Investigation Department (DIC) is in charge of investigating police abuses but was ineffective in addressing impunity or corruption.

An amnesty law covers police and other security personnel involved in "political crimes" committed between 1983 and 2004, except for killings in "cold blood."

The Regional Court of Dakar includes a military tribunal, which has jurisdiction over crimes committed by military personnel. The tribunal is composed of a civilian judge, a civilian prosecutor, and two military assistants to advise the judge, one of whom must be of equal rank to the defendant. The tribunal may try civilians only if they were involved with military personnel who violated military law. The military tribunal provides the same rights as a civilian criminal court.

Arrest Procedures and Treatment of Detainees

Although the law requires warrants issued by judges for police to make an arrest, police often lacked warrants when detaining individuals. The law grants police broad powers to detain prisoners for long periods before filing formal charges. The DIC may hold persons up to 24 hours before releasing or charging them. Authorities did not promptly inform many detainees of the charges against them. Police officers, including DIC officials, may double the detention period from 24 to 48 hours without charge if a prosecutor so authorizes. Investigators may request that a prosecutor double this period to 96 hours. For cases involving claimed threats to state security, the detention period may extend to 192 hours. The detention period does not formally begin until authorities officially declare an individual is being detained, a practice Amnesty International criticized for the resulting lengthy detentions. Bail was rarely available, and officials generally did not allow family access. Except for the first 48 hours of detention, the accused has the right to an attorney, and an attorney is provided at public expense in felony cases to all criminal defendants who cannot afford one after the initial period of detention. Indigent defendants did not always receive attorneys in misdemeanor cases. A number of NGOs provided legal assistance or counseling to those charged with crimes.

Arbitrary Arrest: On April 28, four members of the coalition Non aux APE, including coalition leader Guy Marius Sagna, were arrested while protesting against the signing of an Economic Partnership Agreement between the EU and 16 West African states, the Economic Community of West African States (ECOWAS), and the West African Economic and Monetary Union. Apart from the EU, the country was a member of each organization. On June 3, one day prior to the opening of the annual summit of ECOWAS heads of states and governments in Dakar, authorities arrested eight members of the coalition, including Sagna; on June 6, they were released without charge. Again on September 22, authorities arrested Sagna during another Non aux APE demonstration coinciding with a visit to Dakar by French Prime Minister Manuel Valls. Sagna was released on September 24. In all three instances, authorities allowed demonstrations to proceed but arrested Sagna and others for not complying with police orders for not complying with police orders to vacate certain areas and resisting arrest.

Pretrial Detention: According to a 2014 EU-funded study, more than 60 percent of the prison population consisted of pretrial detainees. The law states an accused person may not be held in pretrial detention for more than six months for minor crimes; however, authorities routinely held persons in custody until a court demanded their release. Judicial backlogs and absenteeism of judges resulted in an average delay of two years between the filing of charges and the beginning of a trial. In cases involving allegations of murder, threats to state security, and embezzlement of public funds, there were no limits on the length of pretrial detention. In many cases pretrial detainees were held for longer than the length of sentence later received.

Detainee's Ability to Challenge Lawfulness of Detention before a Court: Detainees are legally permitted to challenge in court the legal basis or arbitrary nature of their detention and obtain prompt release and compensation if found to have been unlawfully detained; however, this rarely occurred due to lack of adequate legal counsel.

e. Denial of Fair Public Trial

Although the constitution and law provide for an independent judiciary, the judiciary was subject to corruption and government influence. Magistrates noted overwhelming caseloads, lack of adequate space and office equipment, and inadequate transportation, and they openly questioned the government's commitment to judicial independence. According to *Freedom in the World 2016*, "inadequate pay and lack of tenure expose judges to external influences and prevent the courts from providing a proper check on the other branches of government. The president controls appointments to the Constitutional Council." Authorities did not always respect court orders.

Trial Procedures

Defendants enjoy a presumption of innocence and cannot be compelled to testify against themselves or confess guilt. All defendants have the right to a public trial, to be present in court during their trial, to confront and present witnesses, to present evidence, and to have an attorney (at public expense if needed) in felony cases. Defendants have the right to be informed of the charges against them promptly and in detail with free interpretation as necessary from the moment charged through all appeals. They also have the right to sufficient time and facilities to prepare their defense. Nevertheless, case backlogs, lack of legal counsel, judicial inefficiency and corruption, and lengthy pretrial detention undermined these rights.

Evidentiary hearings may be closed to the public and press. Although a defendant and counsel may introduce evidence before an investigating judge who decides whether to refer a case for trial, police or prosecutors may limit their access to evidence against the defendant prior to trial. A panel of judges presides over ordinary courts in civil and criminal cases.

The right of appeal exists in all courts, except for the High Court of Justice. These rights extend to all citizens.

Political Prisoners and Detainees

There were no reports of political prisoners or detainees.

Civil Judicial Procedures and Remedies

Citizens may seek cessation of and reparation for human rights violations in regular administrative or judicial courts. Citizens may also seek administrative remedies by filing a complaint with the ombudsman, an independent authority. Corruption and lack of independence hampered judicial and administrative handling of these cases. At times prosecutors refused to prosecute security officials, and violators often went unpunished. In matters related to human rights, individuals and organizations may appeal adverse decisions to the ECOWAS Court of Justice in Abuja, Nigeria.

f. Arbitrary or Unlawful Interference with Privacy, Family, Home, or Correspondence

The constitution and law prohibit such actions, and there were no reports that the government failed to respect these prohibitions.

g. Abuses in Internal Conflict

The de facto ceasefire in the Casamance has been in effect since 2012, and President Sall continued efforts to resolve the 34-year-old conflict between separatists and government security forces. Both the government and various factions of the MFDC separatist movement accepted mediation efforts led by neutral parties, including Christian and Islamic organizations. Progress toward resolution of the conflict has been incremental.

Killings: Although neither government forces nor MFDC rebels conducted offensive operations in the Casamance during the year, there were several brief, unplanned skirmishes. An undetermined number of MFDC rebels were injured or killed in these encounters.

Abductions: On at least two occasions, individuals believed to be MFDC rebels took hostages, according to local sources. Both incidents were related to acts of banditry.

Section 2. Respect for Civil Liberties, Including:

a. Freedom of Speech and Press

The constitution and law provide for freedom of speech and press, but the government occasionally limited these freedoms.

<u>Freedom of Speech and Expression</u>: Blasphemy, security, and criminal defamation laws are in place and were occasionally enforced.

In October police arrested a French national for making death threats, defamation, and blasphemy. Following his arrest, the accused reportedly admitted to police that he maligned Islam as a "terrorist religion," the Quran as a "book of lies," and the Prophet Muhammad as "the terrorists' guide." In November a court sentenced him to six months in jail for several offenses, including religious insult, criminal breach of trust, and unlawful access to personal electronic data.

In June a court in Kolda sentenced Islamic preacher Ibrahima Seye, arrested in October 2015, to one year's imprisonment for glorifying terrorism, inciting civil disobedience, and religious intolerance. Considering the sentence too light, the prosecutor on October 11 appealed the decision to the Dakar Court of Appeals, which sentenced Seye to 30 months in prison, where he remained at year's end.

<u>Press and Media Freedoms</u>: Independent journalists regularly criticized the government without reprisal. Private, independent publications and government-affiliated media were available in Dakar, although their distribution in rural areas was irregular.

Radio was the most important medium of mass information and source of news due to the high illiteracy rate. There were approximately 200 community, public, and private commercial radio stations. Although an administrative law regulates radio frequency assignments, community radio operators claimed a lack of transparency in the process.

Although the government continued to influence locally televised information and opinion through Radio Television Senegal (RTS), five privately owned television channels broadcast independently. By law the government holds a majority interest in RTS, and the president directly or indirectly controlled selection of all members of the RTS executive staff.

<u>Censorship and Content Restrictions</u>: Journalists occasionally practiced self-censorship, particularly in government-controlled media.

On February 26, police seized files from the premises of *Walf Fadjiri*, an independent media outlet. The files featured a discussion between a journalist and an opposition activist on the March 20 constitutional referendum (see section 3), during which the journalist insinuated the president was using the referendum as a first step to legalize homosexuality. On February 29, police questioned the journalist about the broadcast for 10 hours.

On March 20, the day of the referendum, authorities attempted to shut down *Walf Fadjiri* for allegedly violating the electoral code by announcing election results while the polls remained open. Due to the presence of a crowd outside the station premises, authorities were unable to shut down the station, which continued to broadcast without interruption.

Libel/Slander Laws: The law criminalizes libel. Unlike in previous years, authorities did not use these laws to block or punish critical reporting and commentary.

Internet Freedom

The government did not restrict or disrupt access to the internet or censor online content, and there were no credible reports the government monitored private online communications without appropriate legal authority. According to the International Telecommunication Union, approximately 58 percent of individuals had internet access.

Academic Freedom and Cultural Events

There were no government restrictions on academic freedom or cultural events.

b. Freedom of Peaceful Assembly and Association

Freedom of Assembly

The constitution and law provide for freedom of assembly, but the government sometimes restricted this right. Some groups complained of undue delays in response to authorization requests for public demonstrations. Other groups were denied such authorization.

In February, for example, the government denied authorization to civil society groups calling for a rally in Dakar to campaign for a "no" vote in the March constitutional referendum.

The government forcibly dispersed demonstrators. For example, in January the government used teargas to disperse a demonstration against homosexuality by a coalition of 17 organizations; authorities had earlier denied the group a permit to demonstrate. Police detained 11 participants who defied the ban and subsequently released them without charge.

On October 14, a coalition of opposition parties, the Front for the Defense of Senegal, held a demonstration in Dakar that drew more than 15,000 demonstrators. Prior to the demonstration, the prefect of Dakar granted the coalition permission to march but altered the proposed route, which triggered a clash when police blocked demonstrators from their initially planned route. Police used tear gas to disperse the crowd, a few of whom were detained and subsequently released on October 16. Some demonstrators also were injured, including former prime minister Abdoul Mbaye.

In January members of the main opposition Parti Democratique Senegalaise-- Toussaint Manga, Bocar Niang, Gallo Tall, Aminata Sakho, Djibril Sarr, Daouda Dieye, Pape Fall, and Serigne Ndame Dieng--were released on bail. In February 2015 the eight had been remanded to custody pending trial for participating in an unauthorized public rally.

Freedom of Association

The constitution and law provide for freedom of association, and the government generally respected this right.

c. Freedom of Religion

See the Department of State's *International Religious Freedom Report* at www.state.gov/religiousfreedomreport/.

d. Freedom of Movement, Internally Displaced Persons, Protection of Refugees, and Stateless Persons

The constitution and law provide for freedom of internal movement, foreign travel, emigration, and repatriation, and the government generally respected these rights.

The government cooperated with the Office of the UN High Commissioner for Refugees (UNHCR) and other humanitarian organizations in providing protection and assistance to internally displaced persons (IDPs), refugees, asylum seekers, and stateless persons.

<u>In-country Movement</u>: MFDC banditry and the risk of landmines restricted movement in some parts of the Casamance.

<u>Foreign Travel</u>: The law requires some public employees to obtain government approval before departing the country. Only the military and judiciary enforced this law, however.

Internally Displaced Persons

During the 34-year Casamance conflict, tens of thousands of persons left villages in the region due to fighting, forced removal, and land mines. The government estimated 10,000 IDPs remained in the Casamance. Some international humanitarian assistance agencies estimated the number could be as high as 24,000. During the year IDPs continued to return to their villages.

Protection of Refugees

<u>Access to Asylum</u>: The law provides for the granting of asylum or refugee status, and the government has established a system for providing protection to refugees. Since the president must approve each case, delays of one to two years in granting refugee status remained a problem. The government generally granted refugee status or asylum and provided refugees with food and nonfood assistance in coordination with UNHCR and NGOs.

The government did not offer all asylum seekers due process or security, since appeals filed by denied asylum seekers were examined by the same committee that examined their original case. A denied asylum seeker can be arrested for staying illegally in the country, and those arrested sometimes remained in "administrative detention" for up to three months before being deported.

<u>Durable Solutions</u>: Since 1989 the country has offered temporary protection to Mauritanian refugees, who were dispersed over a large area in the Senegal River valley along the Mauritania border and enjoyed free movement within the country. According to UNHCR, approximately half of the remaining 13,000 Mauritanian refugees in the country have indicated a desire to remain in Senegal permanently. UNHCR and the governments of Senegal and Mauritania were working to find durable solutions for this population.

The government continued to permit generally unsupervised and largely informal repatriation of Casamance refugees returning from The Gambia and Guinea-Bissau.

Section 3. Freedom to Participate in the Political Process

The constitution and law provide citizens the ability to choose their government in free and fair periodic elections held by secret ballot and based on universal and equal suffrage.

Elections and Political Participation

Recent Elections: In March 2012 voters elected Macky Sall to succeed Abdoulaye Wade as president for a seven-year term. In July 2012 Sall's coalition won a majority of seats in the National Assembly. Local NGOs and observers from the EU, African Union, and ECOWAS characterized the elections as generally free and fair.

On March 20, voters approved a referendum on 15 constitutional amendments, the most important of which reduced the length of future presidential terms from seven to five years. Other clauses reaffirmed the presidential limit of two consecutive terms, expanded the size of the constitutional council, permitted the Senegalese diaspora representation in the National Assembly, and created a formal position for the leader of the opposition. President Sall supported the referendum.

Participation of Women and Minorities: No laws limit the participation of women and members of minorities in the political process, and women and minorities participated. In 2010 the government passed a gender parity law requiring the candidate lists of political parties to contain equal numbers of men and women for elected positions at all levels, from city councils to the National Assembly. While the number of women in elected positions has increased, the law has not significantly expanded their role in exercising political authority since it does not apply to party leadership positions or to other important decision-making bodies such as the cabinet and the judiciary. In some regions, including the holy city of Touba, the gender parity law has not been implemented at all.

Section 4. Corruption and Lack of Transparency in Government

The law provides criminal penalties for official corruption, but the government often did not enforce the law effectively. Officials frequently engaged in corrupt practices with impunity. There were reports of government corruption during the year.

Corruption: In May the country's National Anti-Corruption Agency (OFNAC) published it first annual report, which concluded that bribery, misappropriation, abuse of authority, and fraud remained widespread within government institutions, particularly in the health and education ministries, the postal services, and the Transport Administration. OFNAC attributed corruption to inadequate public access to information, dysfunctional internal compliance monitoring, and inadequate control mechanisms. The report singled out two of the president's allies as among the most corrupt. Two months after the report was published, the president dismissed OFNAC president Nafy Ngom Keita, who claimed her dismissal was politically motivated. Authorities countered that Keita's three-year contract had expired.

On June 24, the president officially granted early release to Karim Wade--a former government minister and the son of former president Wade--who was sentenced in 2015 to six years' imprisonment for illicit enrichment. Sall also released two of Wade's associates, Alioune Samba Diasse and Ibrahim Aboukhalil. The government did not release Wade's seized or frozen assets.

The case of Abdoulaye Balde, the mayor of Ziguinchor and a former cabinet minister, remained pending before the Court for the Suppression of Illicit Enrichment (CREI) at year's end. The CREI had frozen Balde's assets in 2015 pending a corruption investigation.

Financial Disclosure: In 2014 the National Assembly passed a law requiring the president, cabinet ministers, speaker and chief financial officer of the National Assembly, and managers of public funds in excess of one billion CFA francs ($1.7 million) to disclose their assets to the National Anticorruption Commission. Failure to comply may result in a penalty amounting to one-quarter of an individual's monthly salary until forms are filed. The president may dismiss appointees who do not comply. Disclosures, except for the president's, made under the law are confidential, and unauthorized release of asset disclosures is a criminal offense. In May, OFNAC released its 2014-15 annual report, which revealed only 52 percent of government officials subject to disclosure (292 out of 565) had complied by the June 2015 deadline. The president, prime minister, speaker of the National Assembly, and all cabinet members had complied; the head of the armed forces, however, had not.

<u>Public Access to Information</u>: The constitution and law provide citizens the right to access government information, but authorities did not follow consistent practices in determining the grounds for nondisclosure, establishing deadlines for responding to requests for information, or charging processing fees. The government did not have an appeals mechanism to review disclosure denials or public outreach activities or training for public officials on the release of government information.

Section 5. Governmental Attitude Regarding International and Nongovernmental Investigation of Alleged Violations of Human Rights

A wide variety of domestic and international human rights groups generally operated without government restriction, investigating and publishing their findings on human rights cases. Government officials were somewhat cooperative but rarely took action to address their concerns.

<u>The United Nations or Other International Bodies</u>: On May 30, the Extraordinary African Chambers (EAC) sentenced former Chadian dictator Hissene Habre to life imprisonment for war crimes, crimes against humanity, torture, and sexual slavery. The EAC is a hybrid court established by the government in collaboration with the African Union, within the country's legal system, to try Habre as well as the other "persons most responsible" for international crimes committed in Chad during Habre's rule. On June 10, Habre's lawyers appealed the decision. No date for hearing the appeal had been set by year's end, and Habre's assets remained frozen. On July 29, the EAC ordered Habre to compensate his victims between 10 million CFA francs ($17,000) and 20 million CFA francs ($34,000) each, depending on the severity of abuse. Three judges--two Senegalese and a presiding judge from Burkina Faso--oversaw the trial, which began in June 2015 and was open to the public and widely covered by local and international press.

<u>Government Human Rights Bodies</u>: The government's National Committee on Human Rights included government representatives, civil society groups, and independent human rights organizations. The committee had authority to investigate abuses but lacked credibility, had limited funding, did not conduct investigations, and last released an annual report in 2001.

Section 6. Discrimination, Societal Abuses, and Trafficking in Persons

Women

<u>Rape and Domestic Violence</u>: The law prohibits rape, which is punishable by five to 10 years' imprisonment. Nevertheless, the government rarely enforced the law, and rape was widespread. The law does not address spousal rape. The law allows the common practice of using a woman's sexual history to defend men accused of rape.

The law criminalizes assaults and provides for punishment of one to five years in prison and a fine. Domestic violence that causes lasting injuries is punishable with a prison sentence of 10 to 20 years. If an act of domestic violence causes death, the law prescribes life imprisonment. Nevertheless, the government did not enforce the law, particularly when violence occurred within the family. Police usually did not intervene in domestic disputes, and most victims were reluctant to go outside the family for redress. Several women's groups and the Committee to Combat Violence against Women and Children (CLVF) reported a rise in violence against women.

NGOs, including the CLVF, criticized the failure of some judges to apply domestic violence laws, citing cases in which judges claimed lack of adequate evidence as a reason to issue lenient sentences. NGOs also criticized the government's failure to permit associations to bring suits on behalf of victims and the lack of shield laws for rape.

Although current statistics on domestic violence were unavailable, a UN study published in 2015 and based on data collected from relevant national services between 2008 and 2010 in eight regions revealed 507 cases in Dakar, 263 in Thies, 279 in Kaolack, 227 in Diourbel, 201 in Louga, 176 in St Louis, 110 in Fatick, and 67 in Kaffrine. The actual incidence of domestic violence, which many citizens considered a normal part of life, was thought to be much higher than the number of cases reported.

The Ministry of Women, Family, and Childhood is responsible for ensuring the rights of women. The Ministry of Justice is responsible for combating domestic violence. The government-run Ginddi Center in Dakar provided shelter to women and girls who were survivors of rape or early and forced marriage, and to street children.

<u>Female Genital Mutilation/Cutting (FGM/C)</u>: The law provides criminal penalties for the perpetration of FGM/C on women and girls, but no cases were prosecuted during the year. According to 2014 data from a foreign government institution, 17 percent of girls below age 15 had been subjected to FGM/C, but the practice

continued to decline. While not commonly inflicted on adult women, almost all girls in the northern Fouta region were victims of FGM/C, as were 60 to 70 percent of girls in the south and southeast. Sealing, one of the most extreme and dangerous forms of FGM/C, was sometimes practiced by the Toucouleur, Mandinka, Soninke, Peul, and Bambara ethnic groups. According to the NGO German Society for International Cooperation, excision, type II, was the form of FGM/C most frequently practiced.

At the community level, the NGO Tostan implemented a community empowerment program against FGM/C in 176 communities in 10 regions.

Sexual Harassment: The law mandates prison terms of five months to three years and fines of 50,000 to 500,000 CFA francs ($85 to $850) for sexual harassment, but the problem was widespread. The government did not effectively enforce the law, and women's rights groups claimed victims of sexual harassment found it difficult, if not impossible, to present sufficient proof for conviction.

Reproductive Rights: The law provides that all couples and individuals have the right to decide the number, spacing, and timing of their children; to manage their reproductive health; and to have access to the means to do so, free from discrimination, coercion, or violence. It also provides for the right to medical services for all women during pregnancy and to a safe delivery. The law considers the right to reproductive health a "fundamental and universal right guaranteed to all individuals without discrimination."

Poor medical facilities constrained observance of these rights, however, particularly in rural areas and in some urban areas, where lack of funds led to the closing of maternity wards and operating rooms. At times cultural norms impeded women's access to information regarding sexual health. Skilled personnel attended approximately 59 percent of births and provided at least some prenatal care in 96 percent of cases, according to 2014 data from a foreign government organization; the maternal mortality ratio was 315 deaths per 100,000 live births, according to 2015 data from the World Health Organization. The Ministry of Health and Social Action estimated most maternal deaths in childbirth were preventable if skilled health personnel and emergency obstetrical services were available. Social and cultural pressures to have large families reportedly led some husbands to ask health workers to terminate the use of contraceptives by their spouses. This reportedly led women to be discreet in the use of contraception. The ministry collaborated with a foreign government to raise the contraceptive prevalence rate from 18 percent in 2012 to 21 percent in 2015, with a goal of 45 percent by 2020.

<u>Discrimination</u>: The law provides for the same legal status and rights for women as for men. Nevertheless, women faced pervasive discrimination, especially in rural areas where traditional customs, including polygyny and discriminatory rules of inheritance, were strongest. The law requires a woman's approval of a polygynous union, but once in such a union, a woman needed neither to be notified nor to give prior consent if the man took another wife. Approximately 50 percent of marriages were polygynous.

The family code's definition of paternal rights also remained an obstacle to equality between men and women. The code considers men to be heads of household, preventing women from taking legal responsibility for their children. In addition, any childhood benefits are paid to the father. Women can become the legal head of household only if the husband formally renounces his authority before authorities or if he is unable to act as head of household.

While women legally have equal access to land, traditional practices made it difficult for women to purchase property in rural areas. Many women had access to land only through their husbands, and the security of their rights depended on maintaining the relationship with their husbands. In addition rural councils--where women often were underrepresented--allocated most land.

Women experienced discrimination in employment (see section 7.d). Women and girls also experienced discrimination in education since those who become pregnant or married young were often pressured to leave school.

The Ministry of Women, Family, and Childhood has a directorate for gender equality that implements programs to combat discrimination.

Children

<u>Birth Registration</u>: Citizenship is acquired by birth or naturalization, but only the father can automatically transmit nationality to legitimate children; the mother can do so only if her husband is stateless. Legitimate children born to Senegalese women with foreign husbands have the option to acquire citizenship between ages 18 and 25. Illegitimate children usually acquire the citizenship of the mother. The law does not make birth declaration mandatory. While birth certificates are required for enrolling children in school and obtaining other civil documents, children generally were allowed to attend elementary school without a birth certificate. According to the UN Population Fund (UNFPA), only 55 percent of

births were registered. Registering births required payment of a small fee and travel to a registration center, which was difficult for many residents of rural areas. A program initiated by Swiss NGO Aid and Action allowed village chiefs in some areas to register births by text messaging.

While children generally could attend primary school without a birth certificate, they needed one to take national exams. In a June 3 press conference, the director of the civil registry at the Ministry of Local Governance in Dakar stated 180,000 primary school students in the regions of Kolda, Tambacounda, Ziguinchor, and Diourbel had not been registered at birth and lacked birth certificates required to apply for national exams. Authorities conducted judicial mass hearings in these regions to issue birth certificates, and all 180,000 students received certificates in the ensuing weeks.

Education: The law provides for tuition-free, compulsory education for children between ages six and 16, although many children did not attend school due to lack of resources or available facilities. Students often had to pay for their own books, uniforms, and other school supplies.

Girls encountered greater difficulties in continuing in school beyond the elementary level. When families could not afford tuition for all children, parents tended to remove daughters from school, and dropout rates were higher among girls. Sexual harassment by school staff and early pregnancy also caused the departure of girls from school. Many parents opted to keep their middle- and high-school-aged daughters home to work or to marry rather than sending them to school, where predatory teachers could ruin their reputations and future marriage prospects. The UN Children's Fund reported schools enrolled 28 percent of boys in secondary education, compared with 22 percent of girls.

Child Abuse: Child abuse was common, particularly among "talibes," students who were sent by their parents to study in Quranic schools, or "daaras." At some daaras, Quranic instructors exploited, physically abused, and forced children to beg on the street. A 2014 daara-mapping study found an estimated 54,800 talibes in the Dakar region alone. Of this number an estimated 30,000 were forced to beg up to five hours per day. A similar mapping during the year in Saint Louis found 14,000 talibes, with more than 9,000 forced to beg, according to Human Rights Watch. Most talibes appeared to be ages five to 10, although some reportedly were as young as two. According to Human Rights Watch, which on July 28 published the report *Senegal: New Steps to Protect Talibes, Street Children*, at least five talibes were killed by their instructors during the first half of the year. Many talibes were chained, regularly beaten, or forced to live in deplorable conditions. Others were ill due to lack of hygiene, nutrition, and medical care. The courts only prosecuted a small number of cases involving death or extreme abuse.

In April police arrested a Quranic instructor after he falsified a death certificate in March to bury a talibe illegally in Dakar's Thiaroye cemetery. The talibe's father had reported his suspicions about his son's death to authorities, and the prosecutor subsequently ordered the body be exhumed and autopsied. Authorities arrested the instructor and the gravedigger, and the case was pending at year's end.

In June police in Touba arrested Oumar Kante, a Quranic instructor accused of beating to death a 13-year-old student in the Dakar suburb of Parcelles Assaines and then attempting to bury the boy's body in Touba. Kante remained in custody awaiting trial at year's end.

In its July report, Human Rights Watch included a January case in which a man in Diourbel allegedly lured four talibes to his home and raped them, the February beating death of a nine-year-old talibe in Louga, and the June discovery of a 12-year-old talibe chained to a wall by police in Saint Louis. In several cases, authorities released Quranic instructors and dropped charges. The majority of reported incidents took place in and around Dakar and Saint Louis.

At the end of June, the president announced a campaign to remove children from the streets, including those forced to beg by their Quranic teachers. Human Rights Watch and the Platform for the Promotion and Protection of Human Rights, a coalition of 40 children's rights organizations, characterized the campaign as "an important step in reforming a deeply entrenched system of exploitation." The groups urged authorities to sustain the momentum with investigations and prosecutions of teachers and others who committed serious violations against children.

<u>Early and Forced Marriage</u>: By law women have the right to choose when and whom they marry, but traditional practices restricted a woman's choice. The law prohibits the marriage of girls younger than age 16, but this law generally was not enforced in most communities where marriages were arranged. Under certain conditions a judge may grant a special dispensation for marriage to a person below the age of consent. According to UNFPA, 33 percent of women between ages 20 and 24 were married before age 18, based on surveys completed between 2000 and 2011.

According to women's rights groups and officials from the Ministry of Women, Family, and Childhood, child marriage was a significant problem, particularly in the more rural areas in the south, east, and northeast. The ministry conducted educational campaigns to address the problem.

Female Genital Mutilation/Cutting (FGM/C): See information for girls under age 18 in women's section above.

Sexual Exploitation of Children: The law provides that convicted sexual abusers of children receive five to 10 years' imprisonment. If the offender is a family member, the maximum is applied. Any offense against the decency of a child is punishable by imprisonment for two to five years and up to 10 years in certain aggravated cases. Procuring a minor for prostitution is punishable by imprisonment for two to five years and a fine of 300,000 to four million CFA francs ($500 to $6,800). If the crime involves a victim younger than 13, the maximum penalty is applied. The law was not effectively enforced.

The minimum age of consensual sex is 18. Due to social pressures and fear of embarrassment, incest remained taboo and often went unreported and unpunished.

Pornography is prohibited, and pornography involving children under age 16 is considered pedophilia and punishable by up to two years' imprisonment and fines of up to 300,000 CFA francs ($500).

Exploitation of women and girls in prostitution was a problem, particularly in the southeast gold-mining region of Kedougou. Although there were no reports of child sex tourism during the year, the country was considered a destination for child sex tourism.

Infanticide or Infanticide of Children with Disabilities: Infanticide, usually due to poverty or embarrassment, continued to be a problem. Domestic workers and rural women working in cities sometimes killed their newborns if they could not care for them. Others, married to men working outside the country, killed their infants out of shame. According to the African Assembly for the Defense of Human Rights, infanticide also occurred when a woman became pregnant with the child of a man from a prohibited occupational caste. In some cases the families of the women shamed them into killing their babies. If police discovered the identity of the mother, she faced arrest and prosecution.

Displaced Children: Many children displaced by the Casamance conflict lived with extended family members, neighbors, in children's homes, or on the streets. According to NGOs in the Casamance, displaced children suffered from the psychological effects of conflict, malnutrition, and poor health.

International Child Abductions: The country is not a party to the 1980 Hague Convention on the Civil Aspects of International Child Abduction. See the Department of State's *Annual Report on International Parental Child Abduction* at travel.state.gov/content/childabduction/en/legal/compliance.html.

Anti-Semitism

There were approximately 100 Jews resident in the country; there were no reports of anti-Semitic acts.

Trafficking in Persons

See the Department of State's *Trafficking in Persons Report* at www.state.gov/j/tip/rls/tiprpt/.

Persons with Disabilities

The law prohibits discrimination against persons with physical, sensory, intellectual, and mental disabilities in employment, education, air travel, and other transportation, access to health care, the judicial system, and the provision of other state services. The government did not enforce these provisions adequately. The law also mandates accessibility for persons with disabilities, but the government did not effectively enforce the law.

The government provided grants, managed vocational training in regional centers, and offered funding for persons with disabilities to establish businesses. Due to a lack of special education training for teachers and facilities accessible to children with disabilities, authorities enrolled only 40 percent of such children in primary school. Anecdotal evidence indicated children with disabilities who did not attend school generally stayed at home and, in some cases, begged on the streets. Support for persons with mental disabilities was not generally available, and incidents of abuse of persons with mental disabilities were common.

Persons with disabilities struggled to access voting sites. A 2012 law reserves 15 percent of new civil service positions for persons with disabilities.

The Ministry for Health and Social Action is responsible for protecting the rights of persons with disabilities.

National/Racial/Ethnic Minorities

Ethnic groups generally coexisted peacefully. In the Casamance incidents of conflict continued to decline between the Diola, the region's largest ethnic group, and the mostly Wolof Senegalese in the north.

Discrimination against individuals of lower castes continued, and intellectuals or businesspersons from lower castes often tried to conceal their caste identity.

Acts of Violence, Discrimination, and Other Abuses Based on Sexual Orientation and Gender Identity

Consensual same-sex sexual activity between adults, referred to in the law as an "unnatural act," is a criminal offense, and penalties range from one to five years' imprisonment and fines of between 100,000 and 1.5 million CFA francs ($170 and $2,500); however, the law was rarely enforced. There are no laws to prevent discrimination based on sexual orientation or gender identity, nor are there hate crime laws that could be used to prosecute crimes motivated by bias against LGBTI persons.

LGBTI persons faced widespread discrimination, social intolerance, and acts of violence. LGBTI individuals were subject to frequent threats, mob attacks, robberies, expulsions, blackmail, and rape. LGBTI activists also complained of discrimination in access to social services.

In March a student at the University of Dakar accused another student of being gay and making an advance in the shower. A student mob subsequently chased the accused student, who ran to a bank and then a campus security office for safety. Police intervened to protect the student from the mob, which later ransacked and burned the bank and security office.

Many victims were too frightened to report abuse, and those who did were sometimes subject to police abuse, including beatings and humiliating treatment. Police in a few cases arbitrarily arrested LGBTI persons, abused them in detention, and did not follow proper investigative procedures. For example, although the law provides for the arrest of persons caught committing an "unnatural act," police sometimes arrested individuals suspected of being gay and detained them for prolonged periods.

In January an appeals judge overturned the convictions of seven men in Guediawaye who had been jailed for "unnatural acts." Police had arrested the individuals without warrant in July 2015, and in August 2015 a trial judge had sentenced the men to six months in prison. According to sources who spoke to Human Rights Watch, no police officers or other witnesses testified against the men at the trial, and the police document provided none of the basic elements for proving a crime, such as details about the alleged sexual acts.

Local NGOs worked actively on LGBTI rights issues, but because of social stigma and laws against homosexuality, they maintained an exceedingly low profile.

Media rarely reported acts of hatred or violence against LGBTI persons.

HIV and AIDS Social Stigma

The law prohibits all forms of discrimination against persons with HIV/AIDS, and the government and NGOs conducted HIV/AIDS awareness campaigns to increase social acceptance of persons with HIV or AIDS. Nevertheless, human rights activists reported HIV-positive individuals and those with AIDS suffered from social stigma due to the widespread belief such status indicated homosexuality. HIV-positive men sometimes refrained from taking antiretroviral drugs due to fear their families would discover their sexual orientation.

Other Societal Violence or Discrimination

In the village of Keur Ibra Niane, Thies region, a mob in July beat to death a man suspected of stealing haystacks. Police subsequently arrested five suspects and referred them to a judge, who remanded them into custody pending further investigation. The case was still pending at year's end.

Section 7. Worker Rights

a. Freedom of Association and the Right to Collective Bargaining

The law provides for the rights of workers to form and join independent unions, except security force members, including police and gendarmes, customs officers, and judges. The law allows civil servants to form and join unions. Before a trade union can exist legally, the labor code requires authorization from the Ministry of

Interior. Unions have no legal recourse if the minister refuses registration. Under the law, as part of the trade union recognition process, the ministry has the authority to check the morality and aptitude of candidates for positions of trade union officials. In addition the law provides that minors (both as workers and as apprentices) cannot organize without parental authorization. The state prosecutor can dissolve and disband trade unions by administrative order if union administrators are not following union regulations for what a union is supposed to be doing on behalf of its members. The law prohibits antiunion discrimination. The law allows unions to conduct their activities without interference and provides for the right to bargain collectively. Foreigners may hold union office only if they have lived in the country for five years and only if his or her country provides the same right to Senegalese citizens. Collective bargaining agreements applied to an estimated 44 percent of union workers. Unions are able to engage in legal proceedings against any individual or entity that infringes the collective bargaining rights of union members, including termination of employment.

The law provides for the right to strike; however, certain regulations restrict this right. The constitution seriously undermines the right to strike by stipulating that a strike must not infringe on the freedom to work or jeopardize an enterprise. The law states workplaces may not be occupied during a strike, whether or not such strike is peaceful, and may not violate nonstrikers' freedom to work or hinder the right of management to enter the premises of the enterprise. This means pickets, go-slows, working to rule, and sit-downs are prohibited. Unions representing members of the civil service must notify the government of their intent to strike at least one month in advance; private-sector unions must notify the government three days in advance. The government does not have any legal obligation to engage with groups who are planning to strike, but the government sometimes engaged in dialogue with these groups. The right to strike is restricted further by the power of authorities to requisition workers to replace those on strike in all sectors, whether or not they are "essential services" sectors. The government effectively enforced applicable laws on the right to strike. Penalties for noncompliance include a fine, imprisonment from three months to one year, or both. Penalties were sufficient to deter violations. The labor code does not apply to the informal sector and thus excludes the majority of the workforce, including subsistence farmers, domestic workers, and those employed in many family businesses.

The government and employers generally respected freedom of association and the right to collective bargaining. Workers exercised the right to form or join unions, but antiunion sentiment within the government was strong. Trade unions organize on an industry-wide basis, very similar to the French system of union organization.

There were no confirmed reports of antiunion discrimination during the year.

b. Prohibition of Forced or Compulsory Labor

The law prohibits all forms of forced or compulsory labor. Although the law prohibits begging for economic gain, a provision of the penal code provides that "the act of seeking alms on days, in places, and under conditions established by religious traditions" does not constitute begging. Many provisions of the law impose imprisonment with compulsory prison labor as a penalty for noncompliance, such as for participation in strikes in "essential services," for occupying the workplace or its immediate surroundings during strike actions, or for breaching labor discipline deemed to endanger ships or the life or health of persons on board.

Following the president's announcement of a campaign against child begging, authorities began removing children from the streets. During the first three months of the campaign, police collected 843 children begging on the streets and sent them to the Ginddi Center, the sole government-run shelter for abused and neglected children in the country. Many of these children were subsequently returned to their families or their daaras based on the child's decision. The practice of forced begging, however, continued largely unabated, and there were no arrests, prosecutions, or convictions in connection with forced begging during the year.

The government did not effectively enforce applicable laws against forced labor, and such practices continued to occur, particularly forced child labor, including forced begging by children in some Quranic schools (see section 6). Some children in these schools (daaras) were kept in conditions of servitude, being forced to work daily, generally in street begging, and had to meet a daily quota for money (or sometimes sugar or rice) set by their teachers.

Also see the Department of State's *Trafficking in Persons Report* at www.state.gov/j/tip/rls/tiprpt/.

c. Prohibition of Child Labor and Minimum Age for Employment

Regulations on child labor set the minimum working age at 15. The law prohibits many forms of hazardous child labor but includes exceptions. In the agricultural sector, for example, children as young as age 12 are permitted to work in a family environment when necessary. The law also allows boys under age 16 to work in underground mines and quarries doing "light work." Due to the nature of the dangers associated with mining, "light work" activities do not prevent exposure to hazards.

Inspectors from the Ministry of Labor are charged with investigating and initiating lawsuits in child labor cases. The ministry's investigators can visit any institution during work hours to verify and investigate compliance with labor laws and can act on tips from trade unions or ordinary citizens.

Labor laws prohibiting child labor were largely unenforced. The Ministry of Labor sent investigators to investigate formal work places, but they were not trained to deal with child labor problems. The Child Labor Division in the Ministry of Labor was severely understaffed and underfunded. Inspectors lacked adequate resources to monitor the informal sector, and no cases of child labor have ever been identified in the formal sector. There was no specific system in place to report child labor violations, largely due to inadequate funding of the Child Labor Division and the Ministry of Labor. The ministry instead relied on unions to report violators. The government conducted seminars with local officials, NGOs, and civil society to raise awareness of the dangers of child labor and exploitive begging.

Most instances of child labor occurred in the informal economy where labor regulations were not enforced. Economic pressures and inadequate educational opportunities often pushed rural families to emphasize work over education for their children. Child labor was especially common in the regions of Tambacounda, Louga, and Fatick, where up to 90 percent of children worked. Child labor was prevalent in many informal and family-based sectors, such as agriculture (millet, corn, and peanuts), fishing, artisanal gold mining, garages, dumpsites, slaughterhouses, salt production, rock quarrying, and metal- and woodworking shops. In the large, informal, unregulated artisanal mining sector, entire families, including children, were engaged in artisanal mining work. Child gold washers, most between ages 10 and 14, worked approximately eight hours a day without training or protective equipment. There were also reports of children working on family farms or herding cattle. Children also worked as domestics, in tailoring shops, at fruit and vegetable stands, and in other areas of the informal economy.

In 2008 (the most recent year for which such data was available) a national child labor survey published by the National Agency of Demography and Statistics measured the economic activities of children during the prior 12 months. According to the survey, 37 percent of children between ages five and 17 worked. A predominant type of forced child labor was the forced begging by children sent to live and study under the supervision of Quranic teachers (see sections 6 and 7.b.). Also see the Department of Labor's *Findings on the Worst Forms of Child Labor* at www.dol.gov/ilab/reports/child-labor/findings/.

d. Discrimination with Respect to Employment and Occupation

The labor law prohibits discrimination in employment and occupation based on national origin, race, sex, disability, and religion; violators are officially subject to fines ranging from 250,000 CFA francs ($426) to one million CFA francs ($1,700) and imprisonment for a period of one month up to one year, but these were not regularly enforced. The law does not explicitly prohibit discrimination based on sexual orientation or gender identity. The government did not effectively enforce the antidiscrimination provisions of the law. Gender-based discrimination in employment and occupation occurred and was the most prevalent form of discrimination. Men and women have equal rights to apply for a job. Women represented 52 percent of the population, but they performed 90 percent of domestic work and 85 percent of agricultural work. The law requires equal pay for equal work, but women experienced discrimination in employment and operating businesses (see section 6).

e. Acceptable Conditions of Work

The national minimum hourly wage was 209 CFA francs ($0.36), but for agricultural workers it was 183 CFA francs ($0.31). The Ministry of Labor is responsible for enforcing the minimum wage. Labor unions also acted as watchdogs and contributed to effective implementation of the minimum wage in the formal sector. The minimum wage provisions apply to foreign and migrant workers as well.

For most occupations in the formal sector, the law mandates a standard workweek of 40 to 48 hours, or 2,080 hours per year, with at least one 24-hour rest period per week, one month per year of annual leave, enrollment in government social security and retirement plans, safety standards, and other measures. Night work is defined as activity between 10 p.m. and 5 a.m.; night workers should receive a supplementary rate of 60 percent for any night hours worked and 100 percent for any night hours worked on holidays. The law does not prohibit excessive or compulsory overtime in the formal sector.

Premium pay for overtime is required only in the formal sector. Legal regulations on occupational safety and health exist, and the government sets the standards.

Employees or their representatives have the right to propose whatever they assume will insure their protection and safety. They can refer to the competent administrative authority in case the employers refuse.

The Ministry of Labor, through the Labor Inspection Office, is responsible for enforcing labor standards in the formal sector; those who violate standards are officially subject to fines ranging from 250,000 CFA francs ($420) to one million CFA francs ($1,700) and imprisonment for a period of one month up to one year, but these were not regularly enforced. Enforcement of the workweek standard was irregular. Labor inspectors had poor working conditions and lacked transportation to conduct their mission effectively. The number of labor inspectors was insufficient to enforce compliance. Violations of wage, overtime, and occupational safety and health standards were common. The minimum wage also covers the informal sector but was not enforced, especially for domestic workers. Due to high unemployment and a slow legal system, workers seldom exercised their nominal right to remove themselves from situations that endangered health or safety. According to government statistics, there were 1,736 cases related to workplace accidents in 2015 (the majority of which took place in Dakar); the reality is likely much higher, as the official number does not take into account the large number of workplace accidents in the informal sector.